EASTER CHANGES

Everything

A 6-WEEK FAMILY DEVOTIONAL
FOR EASTER & BEYOND

ONE BIG STORY

B&H kids

Brentwood TN

To my grandma, Celeste Sledge.
Your devotion to the gospel has changed
everything for me. I love you.
–Lauren

Jesus said to her [Martha],
"I am the resurrection and the life. The one who believes
in me, even if he dies, will live. Everyone who lives
and believes in me will never die. Do you believe this?"
—John 11:25–26

Contents

HOW TO USE THIS DEVOTIONAL

EASTER CHANGED EVERYTHING for Jesus's friends!

For centuries, God's people waited for a Savior to rescue them from the punishment of sin. Since the first people God created, everyone has sinned, and sin has to be punished.

When Jesus died on the cross, He took the punishment of sin that we deserve, and when He rose from the grave, His victory was announced loud and clear! Before His death and resurrection, Jesus taught His friends how to read the Scriptures and prepared them to be teachers too. Now it was time for them to go tell everyone the good news: their Rescuer had come, and He had defeated sin through His death and resurrection!

They were all on a mission to share this good news, *the gospel*, with everyone they met and to show them it had changed their lives.

So how has Easter changed you?

Over the next six weeks, ***read the devotional as a family***. Then, for three days out of the week, perhaps around the dinner table or before you go your separate ways in the morning, ***read the Bible passage*** and ***ask the day's questions***. You may even want to ***write down everyone's answers*** and keep the book to remember how Easter has changed everything for your family too!

THE EASTER STORY

Read this as a family before week 1 begins.
From John 19-20 and Mark 15-16

FOR JESUS'S FRIENDS, Friday was the worst day ever. While Jesus prayed in a garden the night before, their friend Judas walked up to Jesus and kissed Him on the cheek. It might have seemed like a nice gesture at first, but suddenly, guards surrounded Jesus and arrested Him. But for what? Jesus was 33 years old, and He'd never sinned. He'd never lied to His parents, cheated on a test, or betrayed a friend. He certainly hadn't committed a crime. He loved God and people unlike any human had ever done before.

Still, the religious leaders were mad at Jesus for teaching different things than they did, and they wanted Jesus to go away—to die. The soldiers hit Him, made fun of Him, and nailed His hands and feet to a wooden cross, where He hung until He died. It was the worst kind of death imaginable, reserved only for the meanest, most terrible criminals.

But Jesus wasn't a criminal at all. He was the Messiah: God's promised Rescuer. He was fully God, fully human, and the King of God's people. He could have come off the cross and saved Himself, but He didn't.

The religious leaders may have planned for Jesus to die, but God had a bigger plan. Jesus stayed on the cross until He died because He loved the world—even the people who killed Him.

He knew that all sin deserves to be punished by death. Because Jesus was both human and God and because He had never sinned, His sacrifice was the only one that could have taken the punishment for all sin.

After Jesus died, the soldiers took His body down from the cross, and Jesus's heartbroken friends buried Him in a tomb. A stone was rolled in front of the door, and Roman soldiers guarded the tomb so that no one could try to take Jesus's body out of the grave.

Nothing would ever be the same again. It was the worst day ever.

By Sunday, Jesus's friends were still sad and confused. How could their Messiah be dead? How could He rescue God's people if He was in a tomb?

Two of Jesus's friends, both named Mary, walked to where Jesus was buried so that they could wrap His body in linen. But when they arrived, the stone in front of Jesus's tomb had been rolled away, the soldiers were gone, and the tomb was empty. How could this be?

An angel told the women to go tell everyone why Jesus wasn't there anymore: He was alive! It was too good to be true, wasn't it?

But it wasn't. Jesus appeared to one of the women Himself, and she fell at His feet and worshiped Him. He sent her back to the other disciples to share the good news—the best news ever. When Jesus's other friends went to the tomb to see for themselves, it was just as the woman had said: the tomb was empty. Jesus was alive.

Nothing would ever be the same again.

IT WAS THE BEST DAY EVER.

WEEK 1: WHAT'S NEXT?

From Luke 24 and John 20:24-29

How could it be? Two of Jesus's friends, Peter and John, raced to the tomb as fast as their feet would take them. They had just learned that Jesus wasn't in the tomb anymore! Was He alive? Could it be true?

Just two days ago, they saw His lifeless body hanging on the cross. They were there when He was buried in a tomb. Sure, Jesus told them He would die and live again, but wasn't that just one of the stories He'd told? They didn't always understand *everything* He said.

If they were being honest with themselves, they hadn't believed Him. When they arrived at the tomb, everything changed.

He was gone.

Peter and John went back to Jerusalem to tell their friends. They wondered what it could mean.

Where is He? they wondered.

A few days later, everyone knew Jesus's body was gone, and rumors were starting to spread. Jesus's friends were terrified that the people who killed Jesus would come after them too, so they hid in a locked room. That's when they heard a voice. Chill bumps prickled their arms, and everyone went silent. They thought they would never hear that voice again.

It was Jesus!

How could it be?! The door was locked, but He was standing right there!
"Don't be afraid," Jesus said. "It's really me."

He held out His hands so that they could see where the nails held Him to the cross. He wasn't a ghost; He was a real person! He had been dead, and then He was alive! Jesus reminded everyone in the room that this was the plan all along. It had happened just as He said it would.

But why did it have to happen that way? the disciples wondered.

Jesus had told them before—a few times. He'd told them with His words, and He had been telling them through the Bible for thousands of years. No one can ever be good enough to earn their way to God. We are all infected with sin, and we can't get rid of it by ourselves.

God's punishment for sin is death. Only a human who has never been infected by sin can be the sacrifice for sin. Jesus, who is fully God and fully human, is the only human to never, ever be infected by sin. He willingly came to earth to take the punishment for sin.

Any sin? All sin? How could this be? Jesus's friends couldn't believe their ears. Their minds were confused, and their hearts were bursting with awe.

Jesus had been through a lot in the past four days, and His friends had been through a lot too. But Jesus knew that for His friends, this was just the beginning.

Everything had changed.

Day 1

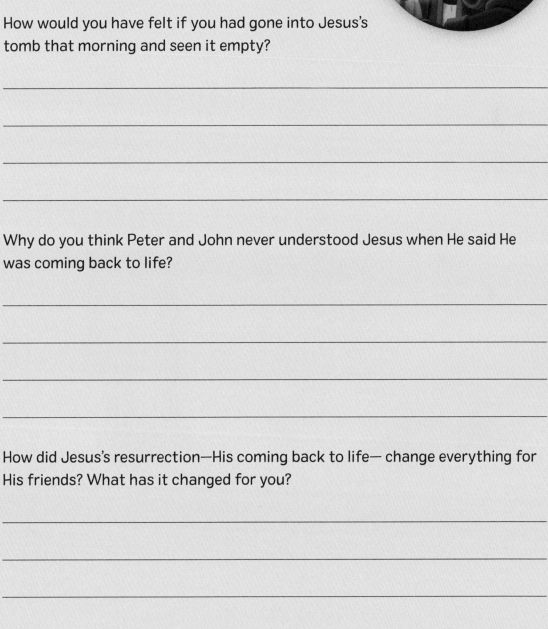

The other disciple, who had reached the tomb first, then also went in, saw, and believed. For they did not yet understand the Scripture that he must rise from the dead. Then the disciples returned to the place where they were staying.—John 20:8–10

How would you have felt if you had gone into Jesus's tomb that morning and seen it empty?

_____

_____

_____

_____

Why do you think Peter and John never understood Jesus when He said He was coming back to life?

_____

_____

_____

_____

How did Jesus's resurrection—His coming back to life— change everything for His friends? What has it changed for you?

_____

_____

_____

_____

Day 2

He told them, "These are my words that I spoke to you while I was still with you—that everything written about me in the Law of Moses, the Prophets, and the Psalms must be fulfilled." . . . He also said to them, "This is what is written: The Messiah would suffer and rise from the dead the third day."—Luke 24:44,46

Imagine you were in the room with Jesus's friends when He appeared. How do you think you would have reacted? Would you have been scared?

_____

_____

_____

_____

Why do you think it matters that Jesus didn't come back as a ghost, but as a living person?

_____

_____

_____

_____

God always planned to rescue His people from sin through Jesus—the Bible says Jesus is the Messiah. How has your life been changed because Jesus is the Messiah?

_____

_____

_____

_____

Day 3

From then on Jesus began to point out to his disciples that it was necessary for him to go to Jerusalem and suffer many things from the elders, chief priests, and scribes, be killed, and be raised the third day.—Matthew 16:21

Jesus had been telling His friends about His death and resurrection for a long time. How do you think they felt when it actually happened?

_____

_____

_____

Do you think Jesus's death and resurrection made Jesus's friends trust Him more? How does it make you trust Him more?

_____

_____

_____

_____

Jesus's disciples knew their lives would never be the same after Jesus was resurrected, but they didn't know exactly what that meant. How has the resurrection changed your life? How do you think your life will continue to change because of the resurrection?

_____

_____

_____

_____

WEEK 2: FOREVER FORGIVENESS

From John 21 and Matthew 28

OVER THE NEXT FORTY DAYS, Jesus kept appearing to His friends and other people who followed Him. He reminded them over and over again that this was real.

"It's really Me!" He told over five hundred of His followers. Jesus had defeated death, and His kingdom had arrived! Still, there was one person with whom Jesus had some unfinished business: Peter.

At Jesus's crucifixion just a few weeks earlier, Peter had messed up big. Peter was one of Jesus's best friends, but when people asked whether he followed Jesus, Peter got scared and lied. Three times, Peter was ashamed of Jesus and said he didn't know Him.

How could Jesus ever forgive me? Peter wondered.

Peter loved Jesus so much, but just like everyone else, Peter's heart was infected with sin.

Sometime after Jesus appeared to the disciples again, Jesus came to Peter at sunrise. Jesus asked him a question: "Peter, do you love Me so much that you would sacrifice yourself for Me?"

Peter was sad. He did love Jesus, but not that long ago, he had been too scared to sacrifice anything for Jesus.

"I love You, Lord," was all Peter could say back.

Jesus knew Peter was sorry and sad about his sin. Peter, who usually boasted about his love for Jesus, admitted his love wasn't as big as it could have been.

Jesus told Peter, "I can use you to lead and care for my people now."

Jesus forgave Peter. Even though Peter was infected with sin, Jesus's sacrifice was big enough to forgive him. When people are sorry for their sins and willing to follow Jesus, Jesus's sacrifice covers their sins—big and small. His forgiveness is good enough for it all.

At the end of forty days, Jesus announced, "It's time for me to go back to my Father."

He was leaving again?!

Jesus's friends couldn't believe it. He had just gotten back! How could Jesus leave if His kingdom was here? Shouldn't He take His rightful place on a throne somewhere?

It's true. Jesus was already King, but He wasn't the King everyone expected. Jesus's kingdom was spiritual, and it was more powerful than any other kingdom or throne ever to exist. He is a King with the power to do things like heal the sick and raise the dead to life and, most importantly, forgive sin. Even though Jesus's kingdom was spiritual, Jesus told His friends that it would one day be physical. Jesus would destroy all the bad things and make all the good things last forever.

"But it's not time for that yet," Jesus told His friends. "Wait for the Holy Spirit to come to you. When He does, He will give you the power to tell everyone that God forgives sin, to baptize them, and to teach them the things I taught you. Don't worry—I will be with you."

As Jesus's friends kept their eyes on Jesus, His body rose through the clouds until He couldn't be seen anymore.

Jesus's friends were amazed.

What's next? they wondered.

BUT JESUS HAD JUST TOLD THEM.

Day 1

He asked him the third time, "Simon, son of John, do you love me?"

He said, "Lord, you know everything; you know that I love you."

"Feed my sheep," Jesus said. . . . After saying this, he told him, "Follow me."—John 21:17,19

How do you feel after you wrong someone?

_____

_____

_____

_____

How do you think Peter felt when Jesus kept asking whether Peter loved Him?

_____

_____

_____

_____

Have you ever wondered, *How could Jesus forgive me?* How In your own words, describe how Jesus forgives people.

_____

_____

_____

_____

Day 2

Therefore, as God's chosen ones, holy and dearly loved, put on compassion, kindness, humility, gentleness, and patience, bearing with one another and forgiving one another if anyone has a grievance against another. Just as the Lord has forgiven you, so you are also to forgive.—Colossians 3:12–13

When Jesus forgave Peter, what did He teach us about forgiveness?

_____

_____

_____

_____

When was the last time someone forgave you? How did it make you feel to be forgiven?

_____

_____

_____

_____

The book of Colossians says that because Jesus has forgiven us, we can forgive other people. When was the last time you forgave someone? Is there anyone you need to forgive today?

_____

_____

_____

_____

_____

Day 3

He said to them, "It is not for you to know times or periods that the Father has set by his own authority. But you will receive power when the Holy Spirit has come on you, and you will be my witnesses in Jerusalem, in all Judea and Samaria, and to the end of the earth."—Acts 1:7–8

How do you think Jesus's friends felt when Jesus said He had to leave again?

_____

_____

_____

_____

Jesus's friends didn't understand everything He taught them. What are some things in the Bible you don't understand?

_____

_____

_____

_____

Jesus told His friends to tell everyone about Him. Whom can you tell about Jesus, and when do you plan to do that?

_____

_____

_____

WEEK 3: A PROMISE KEPT

From Acts 2

HE WAS GONE—AGAIN. Once they were sure He wouldn't come back down with a belly laugh and a "just kidding!," Jesus's friends slowly made their way back to Jerusalem.

"The Holy Spirit will come to you," He'd said. All they could do was trust Jesus. So they waited and regrouped. Jesus had kept all His promises so far. He could be trusted to keep them again.

A week later. . .

Nothing had happened.

Lots of Jesus's friends and followers were together in a house celebrating the Day of Pentecost, an annual Jewish holiday. They were celebrating, but really, they were waiting and waiting and waiting for what Jesus said would happen.

Suddenly, a sound WHOOSHED through the group of friends! Everyone was startled, but when they looked around, they each had something like flames of fire resting on them. The flames didn't burn. They were in awe, and when they started talking to each other, they were all speaking different languages!

People from all over the world—people from different countries, who each spoke different languages—had come to Jerusalem for Pentecost too. When they heard the *whoosh*, they gathered close to the door.

The Holy Spirit had come and filled the disciples, just like Jesus promised. They ran outside the house to where the visitors were.

The visitors, who spoke many different languages, were confused when they understood everything everyone was saying. How could Jesus's friends know so many languages?

They didn't, but the Holy Spirit was helping them. They told the visitors all the amazing things God had done. They told them how God saves sinners,

and they shared what Jesus had taught them. Some of the visitors were amazed and believed everything the disciples said.

Other people thought they were just plain crazy.

Peter knew exactly what was going on. How could they ever have doubted Jesus would keep His promise?

"Everyone, listen up," Peter shouted to the crowd. "These people aren't crazy! The prophets told us God would pour out His Spirit on His people and that everyone who calls on the name of the Lord will be saved!

"You see, our teacher, Jesus of Nazareth, is the Son of God! It was you who put Him to death, but did you know God raised Him from the dead? He changed everything. Jesus is the Messiah, the Rescuer! Now, all you have to do is turn away from your sins and follow Jesus. Believe in Him, and you will be saved."

And they were.

That day, three thousand people heard the good news in their languages, and they believed. Jesus's friends baptized them,

AND THEY WERE FOREVER CHANGED.

Day 1

"Then they were all filled with the Holy Spirit and began to speak in different tongues, as the Spirit enabled them."—Acts 2:4

Imagine you were with the disciples when the flames came and rested on everyone. How do you think you would have reacted?

_____

_____

_____

_____

How do you think the disciples felt when they realized Jesus had kept His promise to send the Holy Spirit?

_____

_____

_____

_____

The Holy Spirit empowered God's people to share the gospel, the good news about Jesus. Have you ever shared the gospel with anyone? What was that like?

_____

_____

_____

_____

Day 2

Peter replied, "Repent and be baptized, each of you, in the name of Jesus Christ for the forgiveness of your sins, and you will receive the gift of the Holy Spirit."—Acts 2:38

Peter shared the good news that Jesus died and rose from the grave to thousands of people on the Day of Pentecost. Who shared that good news with you for the first time? Do you remember what it felt like when you first believed in Jesus?

_____

_____

_____

_____

How do you think the people felt when they realized that Jesus, who they probably thought was a criminal, was God?

_____

_____

_____

_____

Do you think Peter was nervous when he preached that day? Why or why not? How do you think God helped him as he spoke to everyone?

_____

_____

_____

_____

Day 3

Now God has revealed these things to us by the Spirit, since the Spirit searches everything, even the depths of God.—1 Corinthians 2:10

Did you know the Holy Spirit is God? Read John 16:7. How does it make you feel to know that Christians today have the Holy Spirit?

_____

_____

_____

_____

The Holy Spirit can help us understand things we don't understand! What are some things that confuse you about the Bible? Pray together that the Holy Spirit will help you understand.

_____

_____

_____

_____

Peter boldly shared the good news of Jesus because the Holy Spirit helped him. What is something bold the Holy Spirit could help you do? Why is it sometimes hard to share about Jesus?

_____

_____

_____

WEEK 4: THE UNLIKELIEST CHRISTIAN

From Acts 9:1–30

AFTER PENTECOST, people everywhere started believing in Jesus and calling themselves Christ-followers or "followers of the Way." The Christ-followers gathered in small groups called churches. But not everyone liked the churches. Some of Jesus's own people, the Jews, thought Jesus was a liar and a false teacher. They didn't believe God had sent Jesus to take the punishment for their sins.

One Jewish teacher named Saul persecuted Jesus's followers. He arrested them and sometimes even killed them. Saul hated Jesus and Jesus's followers, and he wanted to stop them—now! No one despised Christ-followers more than Saul.

One day, Saul was on his way to a town called Damascus to arrest some people from the churches.

"Serves them right!" Saul grumbled to his friends who were with him.

While they were traveling, a bright light flashed around Saul, blinding him and knocking him to the ground. A voice called from heaven, "Saul, Saul! Why are you persecuting me?"

Saul couldn't see a thing. He was very confused.

"Who are you?" Saul cried.

"I am Jesus. Now go to where you were going and learn what to do next."

Jesus? How can it be? Saul wondered. He thought Jesus had been killed on a cross, so how could He be calling to Saul from the sky? Saul didn't know what was happening, but he knew something *big* had just happened—maybe the biggest thing ever.

After the light disappeared, Saul still couldn't see. The men who were with him had to guide him all the way to Damascus.

God told a Christ-follower in Damascus named Ananias that Saul was on his way. God wanted Ananias to share the gospel, or the good news that Jesus had died and raised from the dead, with Saul. *SAUL?!* Ananias thought. *Isn't this the man who hurts followers of the Way?? Won't he want to hurt me?*

Ananias was right to be afraid. Saul was one of the meanest and scariest people to Jesus's followers. Still, God told Ananias not to be afraid. God was going to use Saul to spread the good news of Jesus to everyone in the world. Jesus had sacrificed Himself for even the meanest, scariest people, and God was going to forgive Saul's sins.

Ananias obeyed God. When Saul arrived, Ananias prayed with him, and God brought Saul's sight back. Saul could see everything. He could especially see that he had been wrong to hurt Christ-followers. He could see Jesus was the Son of God. Saul was sorry for his sins, and he wanted to follow Jesus.

Saul, the man who hated Jesus's followers, began to follow Jesus.

Saul got baptized and immediately started learning from the people in the churches he had wanted to hurt just a few days before.

It may have been the unlikliest baptism ever.

How can this be? some followers wondered. *Isn't this the man who used to hurt us?*

Saul had done many terrible things to Christ-followers, but anyone who believes in Jesus can receive forgiveness—even the unlikeliest person.

When Jesus died on the cross and was raised from the dead, He changed everything.

SAUL WAS READY TO TELL EVERYONE.

Day 1

Now Saul was still breathing threats and murder against the disciples of the Lord. He went to the high priest and requested letters from him to the synagogues in Damascus, so that if he found any men or women who belonged to the Way, he might bring them as prisoners to Jerusalem. —Acts 9:1–2

What's the worst, most unimaginable sin you can think of? Do you believe God would forgive that? Why or why not?

_____

_____

_____

_____

How do you think you would feel if you knew someone like Saul was coming to your hometown to arrest Christians?

_____

_____

_____

_____

When Saul was planning to hurt people, God was planning to rescue him. How does it make you feel to know God can and does forgive the meanest, unlikeliest people?

_____

_____

_____

Day 2

Falling to the ground, he heard a voice saying to him, "Saul, Saul, why are you persecuting me?"

"Who are you, Lord?" Saul said.

"I am Jesus, the one you are persecuting," he replied. "But get up and go into the city, and you will be told what you must do."—Acts 9:4–6

Why do you think God chose to rescue Saul from sin and death even before Saul was sorry for what he had done?

_____

_____

_____

_____

Imagine you were Ananias and God told you to go help Saul. Would you have done it immediately? What questions would you have had for God?

_____

_____

_____

_____

Who is someone you know who is unlikely to follow Jesus? Make a plan to share the good news about Jesus with them. Start praying for God to save that person.

_____

_____

_____

Day 3

But the Lord said to him [Ananias], "Go, for this man is my chosen instrument to take my name to Gentiles, kings, and Israelites. I will show him how much he must suffer for my name."... Immediately he began proclaiming Jesus in the synagogues: "He is the Son of God."—Acts 9:15, 20

God planned to use Saul to tell all kinds of people about Himself. Why is it so powerful that God chose Saul for this task?

_____

_____

_____

_____

Would you have had a hard time believing Saul was truly following Jesus? Why or why not?

_____

_____

_____

_____

The Bible says that when people believe in Jesus, it's like they can see for the first time. Do you remember the first time you believed in Jesus? What was something you could see for the first time?

_____

_____

_____

From Acts 15; 27,28

THE HOLY SPIRIT was changing Saul's life. Saul started going to synagogues to share the good news that Jesus had changed everything. "We can never be good enough to earn our way to God! Believe in Jesus, and your sins can be forgiven, just like mine!"

In the same places where Saul had once proclaimed that Jesus was a fraud and Jesus's followers were lying, he now shouted, "Jesus is Lord!"

Many people hated Saul's message—especially Saul's friends who had per-secuted Christ-followers with him. Just like they wanted to stop the Christ-followers from telling anyone else about Jesus, they wanted to stop Saul.

But Saul learned and grew even more confident in sharing his message—doing whatever he could do to get the message through to different kinds of people. He even went by his non-Jewish name, Paul, when he talked with friends who weren't Jewish.

Paul noticed not all people thought everyone deserved to be forgiven. Some people thought a person had to be born a Jew to receive Jesus's sacrifice, or, they had to convert to Judaism before they could follow Jesus.

Paul wanted everyone to know Jesus had come for anyone who believes in Him—not just Jews. No one could do anything to earn their way to God. Paul started traveling everywhere to tell the Gentiles (non-Jewish people) that Jesus's sacrifice was for them too!

He was serious about taking the gospel everywhere.

Paul got on ships and sailed through stormy seas to places where no one had ever heard of Jesus. He stood in towns, knowing the people would throw him out.

He was arrested over and over again. People even tried to kill him for talking about Jesus so much.

Nothing could stop Paul because God was using him.

Because of Paul, thousands of people believed, and the good news that Jesus is King kept spreading. Churches were popping up all over. People no one had expected to follow Jesus began to believe that, because of Jesus's death and resurrection, their sins could be forgiven.

Even though God was using Paul to spread the good news everywhere, Paul's life was hard. The day Jesus stopped him on the road to Damascus was the day Paul went from being a respected, powerful teacher to being hated by all the people who used to love him.

What could possibly make someone endure so much hatred and loneliness? What could make someone want to spend years in prison, knowing he would eventually be killed for sharing this message?

How did Paul keep going?

Paul kept sharing the good news because Jesus had changed him. And through Paul,

GOD CHANGED THE WORLD.

Day 1

And yet because we know that a person is not justified by the works of the law but by faith in Jesus Christ, even we ourselves have believed in Christ Jesus. This was so that we might be justified by faith in Christ and not by the works of the law, because by the works of the law no human being will be justified.
—Galatians 2:16

Paul wanted everyone to know Jesus is Lord—He is the only way to be right with God. What does it mean to be "right" with God?

_____

_____

_____

_____

Has anyone ever told you to stop talking about Jesus? How did that make you feel?

_____

_____

_____

Is it easy or hard to believe *anyone* can be forgiven by Jesus? Do you ever struggle to believe certain people can follow Jesus?

_____

_____

_____

_____

Day 2

Who is weak, and I am not weak? Who is made to stumble, and I do not burn with indignation? If boasting is necessary, I will boast about my weaknesses.
—2 Corinthians 11:29–30

Paul experienced a lot of hard things while he shared about Jesus. Why do you think he kept sharing?

_____

_____

_____

_____

Why do you think Paul said, "I will boast about my weaknesses"?

_____

_____

_____

_____

What is the hardest thing you have ever been through? When you feel weak, whom can you *always* trust to be strong?

_____

_____

_____

_____

_____

Day 3

Paul stayed two whole years in his own rented house. And he welcomed all who visited him, proclaiming the kingdom of God and teaching about the Lord Jesus Christ with all boldness and without hindrance.—Acts 28:30–31

Have you ever wanted to tell someone about Jesus but then felt afraid? What happened?

_____

_____

_____

_____

The Bible says Paul shared about Jesus "without hindrance," which means without stopping. How do you think he did that?

_____

_____

_____

_____

Paul welcomed people into his home and shared the gospel with them. Whom can you welcome into your home, and how can you tell that person about Jesus?

_____

_____

_____

_____

WEEK 6: THE BEST DAY FOREVER

From Revelation 1, 5, 21, 22

THE GOOD NEWS about Jesus's death and resurrection spread like wildfire. Jesus's friends told everyone they met, and those people told people, and they told more people until tens of thousands believed Jesus is King!

Jesus's friends never stopped telling this good news, no matter how much they were threatened. The leaders in their land wanted them to stop spreading the news about Jesus—it was getting out of control! One by one, Jesus's friends were hurt and even killed for spreading the news about Jesus.

Except for John.

John was one of Jesus's friends. He ran to the tomb with Peter. He was one of the first to see that Jesus wasn't there anymore, and he told everyone about it. After years of sharing the good news, John was sent away to a lonely island. His punishment was that he had to keep living, but he couldn't tell people about Jesus anymore. There was no one there to tell.

John thought his days of sharing Jesus's good news were over. Forever.

But while John was sitting all alone, Jesus appeared to John and gave him a vision!

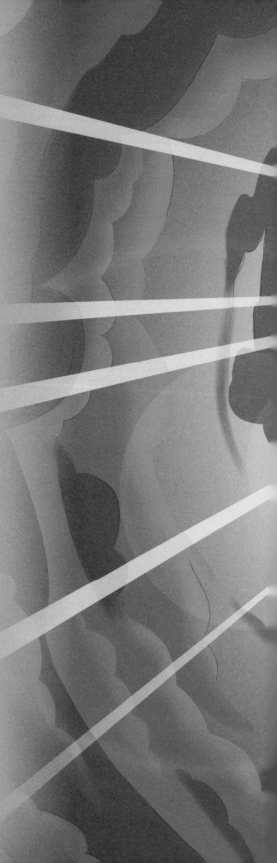

With nothing but time on his hands, John wrote down everything he saw and everything Jesus told him in a letter to Christ-followers. He wrote something a little like this:

"Jesus has given me a revelation! He is King, and He is coming back to establish His kingdom and reunite people with God forever.

"Turn from your sins, and trust Jesus! Live to please God, no matter what happens to you. The people who hurt you and call you frauds and liars aren't your real enemies.

"There is a spiritual enemy named Satan who is far worse than any scary human. He is the one who tempted Adam and Eve with sin, and he has an evil army. Since the very beginning of time, God planned to destroy Satan and the sin that lives inside people.

"Sin must be punished by death. If we took the punishment for our own sins, we would die a forever kind of death. But Jesus is fully God and fully human, and He sacrificed Himself for us like a lamb. He took our punishment and then came back to life. When Jesus died on the cross, He took the punishment for humanity. When He rose from the grave on Easter, He showed us that death can be put to death.

"The hard days aren't over, though. There will be tears and heartache and pain. People may be mean to your families or hurt your friends."

"When Jesus comes and makes His spiritual kingdom physical, He will make everything right. It'll be like the first garden, where Adam and Eve walked with God, but even better. Jesus is going to destroy the enemy, and sin and death will be gone forever. He will wipe away every tear and end every heartache. Pain will be gone for good.

"When Jesus comes back as King, He will make all things new. His rescue mission will be complete. His people will be reunited with God forever.

"Nothing will ever be the same again.

IT'LL BE THE BEST DAY—FOREVER."

Day 1

John: To the seven churches in Asia. Grace and peace to you from the one who is, who was, and who is to come, and from the seven spirits before his throne, and from Jesus Christ, the faithful witness, the firstborn from the dead and the ruler of the kings of the earth.

To him who loves us and has set us free from our sins by his blood, and made us a kingdom, priests to his God and Father—to him be glory and dominion forever and ever. Amen.—Revelation 1:4–6

How does John describe Jesus in Revelation 1:4–6? Which of these descriptions do you have questions about?

_____

_____

_____

_____

John says Jesus makes His people into a kingdom. What do you think that means?

_____

_____

_____

How is Jesus the King of your life already? How does it make you feel that Jesus will be King forever?

_____

_____

_____

Day 2

And they sang a new song:

You are worthy to take the scroll and to open its seals, because you were slaughtered, and you purchased people for God by your blood from every tribe and language and people and nation. You made them a kingdom and priests to our God, and they will reign on the earth.—Revelation 5:9–10

John says Jesus was slaughtered, like a lamb. How does it make you feel to know that Jesus willingly died for you and took the punishment for your sin?

_____

_____

_____

What does Jesus's sacrifice change about the way you live your everyday life?

_____

_____

_____

_____

Because of Christians like John who faithfully shared the gospel, we can know and believe the good news about Jesus today. Who was the first person who ever shared the gospel with you? Whom can you share the gospel with?

_____

_____

_____

_____

Day 3

"Look, I am coming soon! Blessed is the one who keeps the words of the prophecy of this book."

. . . Amen! Come, Lord Jesus!

The grace of the Lord Jesus be with everyone. Amen.
—Revelation 22:7, 20–21

How does it make you feel to know that Jesus is coming back soon?

_____

_____

_____

_____

If Jesus is coming soon, what are some things we can do to get ready for Him?

_____

_____

_____

Because we believe in Jesus's death and resurrection, we are made right with God forever and ever. After reading these stories and answering these questions, how do you think Easter has changed your life?

_____

_____

_____

_____

SIX-WEEK CHALLENGE

EASTER CHANGED EVERYTHING for Jesus's friends. After six weeks of stories and family conversations, hopefully you know how Easter changes everything for your family too!

Keep reading and thinking about how you will follow Jesus as a family. Once a week for the next six weeks, ask the questions below, read the verses, and plan together as a family to follow Jesus in every part of your lives.

At the end of those six weeks, keep reading the Bible and discussing it with your family on your own!

*Week 1: How does Easter change
your involvement in the local church?*

Ephesians 2:18–22   Colossians 3:12–17   Hebrews 10:19–25

Make a plan this week for how your family can invest in your church more.

_____

_____

_____

_____

_____

_____

_____

_____

_____

_____

Week 2: How does Easter change your family life?

Deuteronomy 6:4–9   *Galatians 6:1–10*   *1 John 1:1–7*

Make a plan this week for how your family can spend more time following Jesus together.

_____

_____

_____

_____

_____

_____

_____

_____

_____

_____

_____

_____

_____

Week 3: How does Easter change the way you serve people around you?

Matthew 22:37–40   Mark 9:33–37   1 Peter 4:10

Make a plan this week for how your family can serve others more, both together and individually.

_____

_____

_____

_____

_____

_____

_____

_____

_____

_____

_____

Week 4: How does Easter change the way you read the Bible?

Psalm 1   Psalm 119:9–16   Romans 15:4–5

Make a plan this week for how each of you can read the Bible more consistently.

_____

_____

_____

_____

_____

_____

_____

_____

_____

_____

_____

_____

_____

_____

_____

_____

Week 5: How does Easter change the way you pray?

Matthew 6:5–14   *Romans 8:24–27*   *Ephesians 6:18*

Make a plan this week for how you can pray individually and together as a family more often.

_____

_____

_____

_____

_____

_____

_____

_____

_____

_____

_____

_____

_____

Week 6: How does Easter change the way you share the gospel?

Matthew 28:19–20   Mark 16:15–16   Romans 10:13–14

Make a plan this week for how you can share the gospel more, both as a family and individually.

_____

_____

_____

_____

_____

_____

_____

_____

_____

_____

_____

THE GOSPEL
God's plan for us

The gospel is the good news, the message about Christ, the kingdom of God, and salvation. Use these prompts to share the gospel with your kids.

1. GOD RULES.
Ask: "Who is in charge at home?" Explain that because God created everything, He is in charge of everything. *Read Revelation 4:11.*

2. WE SINNED.
Ask: "Have you ever done something wrong?" Tell kids that everyone sins, or disobeys God. Our sin separates us from God. *Read Romans 3:23.*

3. GOD PROVIDED.
Explain that God is holy and must punish sin. God sent His Son, Jesus, to take the punishment we deserve. *Read John 3:16.*

4. JESUS GIVES.
Ask: "What is the best gift you've ever received?" Say that Jesus took our punishment for sin by giving His life, and He gives us His righteousness. God sees us as if we lived the perfect life Jesus lived. This is the best gift ever! *Read 2 Corinthians 5:21.*

5. WE RESPOND.
Explain that everyone has a choice to make. Ask: "Will you trust Jesus as your Savior and Lord? You can turn from self and sin and turn to Jesus." *Read Romans 10:9-10.*